Neighborhood Walk

Suburb

Peggy Pancella

Heinemann Library
Chicago, Illinois

© 2006 Heinemann Library
a division of Reed Elsevier Inc.
Chicago, Illinois

Customer Service   888–454–2279

Visit our website at www.heinemannlibrary.com

Photo research by Jill Birshbach
Designed by Joanna Hinton-Malivoire and Q2A Creative
Printed in China by South China Printing Co.

10 09 08 07 06
10 9 8 7 6 5 4 3 2

Library of Congress Cataloging-in-Publication Data
Pancella, Peggy.
  Suburb / Peggy Pancella.
     p. cm. -- (Neighborhood walk)
  Includes bibliographical references and index.
  ISBN 1-4034-6219-4 (hc) -- ISBN 1-4034-6225-9 (pb)
  1. Suburbs--United States--Juvenile literature. 2. Suburban life--United
States--Juvenile literature. I. Title. II. Series.
  HT352.U6P37 2006
  307.76'0973--dc22
                                      2005010760

Acknowledgments
The author and publisher are grateful to the following for permission to reproduce copyright material:
Corbis pp. 14, 15; Getty Images pp. 12 (Geostock/PhotoDisc), 17 (News/Tim Boyle), 19 (Image Bank/Larry Daqle Gordon); Heinemann Library pp. 6 (Greg Williams), 7 (Greg Wiliams), 10 (Greg Williams), 16 (Greg Williams), 18 (Greg Williams), 20 (Greg Williams), 21 (Greg Williams), 22 (Greg Williams), 24 (Greg Williams), 25 (Robert Lifson), 28 (Robert Lifson); Photo Edit, Inc. 4 (right, Spencer Grant), 4 (left, Jeff Greenberg), 5 (right, Frank Siteman), 5 (left, Gary Conner), 8 (Rudi Von Briel), 9 (Tom Carter), 11 (Bill Aron), 13 (Tony Freeman), 23 (Tom Prettyman), 26 (Myrleen Ferguson Cate), 27 (Kathy Ferguson-Johnson), 29 (Deborah Davis)

Cover photograph reproduced with the permission of Getty Images (Stone/John Humble)

Every effort has been made to contact copyright holders of any material reproduced in this book. Any omissions will be rectified in subsequent printings if notice is given to the publisher.

Some words are shown in bold, **like this**. You can find out what they mean by looking in the glossary.

Contents

Let's Visit a Suburb

People everywhere live in **neighborhoods**. A neighborhood is a small part of a larger **community**, such as a city or town. A neighborhood's people and places help to make it special.

Some neighborhoods are parts of suburbs.
A suburb is a community that is near a city.
Suburbs are smaller and less crowded than
cities. A city and the suburbs around
it make up a **metropolitan area**.

Homes

Suburbs have many different kinds of homes, but most people in suburbs live in houses. Some houses are very large, and others are quite small. Many houses have yards where people can play and relax.

Houses in suburbs can be spread out.

This apartment building has room for several families.

Some people in suburbs live in **town houses** or apartments. These homes often do not have large yards. They may have shared play areas instead. People can also use **neighborhood** parks or playgrounds.

Getting Around

Many suburbs have special places to ride bikes.

Places in suburbs are usually spread out. Many people use cars to get around. Some people also use **public transportation**. Others walk or ride bikes for short trips.

Many people in suburbs drive into the city to work, shop, or attend special events. They may also ride on buses, trains, or **subways**. Some people **carpool** with others to save money and avoid traffic.

People travel to the city in many different ways.

Schools

Many families with children live in the suburbs. Suburbs need to have many schools for all of these children. Most **neighborhoods** have at least one school.

Some school buildings are tall. Others are more spread out.

Gray M. Sanborn
SCHOOL
101 NORTH OAK St.

Schools in suburbs often have room for large playgrounds.

Schools in suburbs are often one or two stories tall. They usually have play areas nearby. Some children can walk or ride bikes to school. Others ride in cars or school buses.

Working

Many people in suburbs work in the city. Some work in offices or **government** buildings. Others work in stores, restaurants, or factories.

Many workers travel to the city every day.

Some suburbs have large office buildings.

Many people work in the suburbs, too. Suburbs have many of the same kinds of businesses that cities do. Some workers build and repair the roads and buildings that the suburb needs.

13

Keeping Safe

Many workers help keep the suburb safe. Some police officers **patrol** the suburb in cars. Others walk or ride bikes. They try to get to know the people in the **community**.

Police use bikes to get to places where cars cannot go.

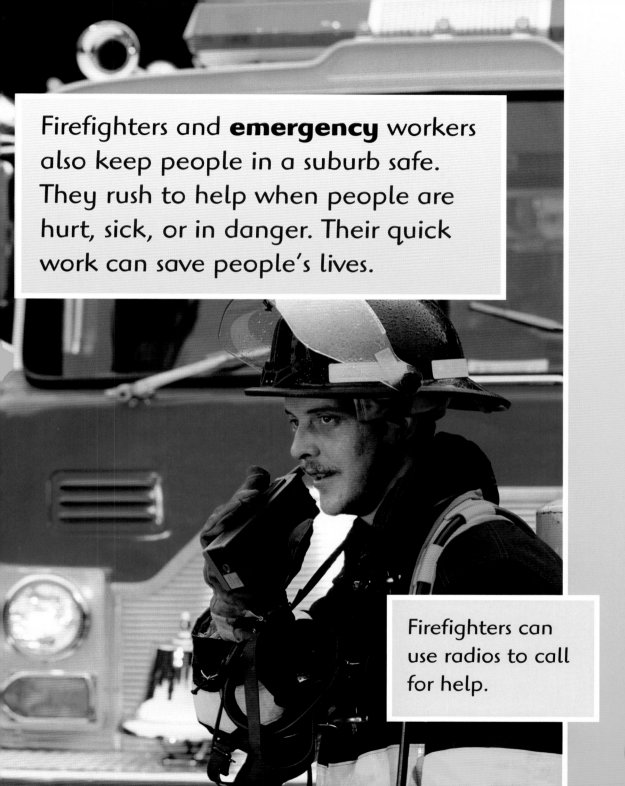

Firefighters and **emergency** workers also keep people in a suburb safe. They rush to help when people are hurt, sick, or in danger. Their quick work can save people's lives.

Firefighters can use radios to call for help.

Shopping

Some suburbs have large shopping centers called **malls**. Malls have many different kinds of stores in one spot. People can buy all kinds of things here. They do not have to drive from place to place to get what they need.

Malls often have stores on more than one level.

Strip malls have several different kinds of stores.

Suburbs have many other stores, too. Some are large and sell many kinds of things. Others are small and sell special products. These stores may be grouped together in a **strip mall** along a main road.

Food

Some grocery stores stay open all day and night.

Most people in suburbs get their food from grocery stores. Large grocery stores sell many kinds of food and other items. Some suburbs also have gardens, **farmers' markets**, or small food shops.

Suburbs have many places to eat as well. People can sit inside a restaurant to eat or pick up food to take home. Some restaurants serve foods from different countries.

Restaurants serve all kinds of foods.

Libraries

Most suburbs have libraries for people to use. People can borrow books and look up information. They can also join book clubs, use computers, or attend special events.

PALATINE
PUBLIC LIBRARY

TOP TEN AGAIN!
Ranked 8th In Nation

Libraries in suburbs may be large or small.

20

Some libraries have special areas for children.

A large suburb may have several libraries or one main library. **Neighborhoods** have smaller **branch** libraries close to where people live. Branch libraries share books and materials from the main library.

Money and Mail

People can use bank machines without getting out of their cars.

Suburbs have banks to handle people's money. Most **neighborhoods** have at least one **branch** bank. People may do business inside a bank. They may also use a drive-up window or **ATM**.

Most neighborhoods have post offices, too. People can mail letters and packages inside. Machines and workers sort the mail. Then letter carriers deliver it.

Letter carriers drive or walk through neighborhoods to deliver the mail.

Other Places in a Suburb

Suburbs need many different kinds of buildings. In a **city hall**, **government** leaders make plans and rules for the suburb. Some suburbs also have **courts** to deal with people who break laws.

PALATINE PARK DISTRICT
250 E. WOOD ST.

Palatine Park District

People meet here to make plans for a suburb's parks.

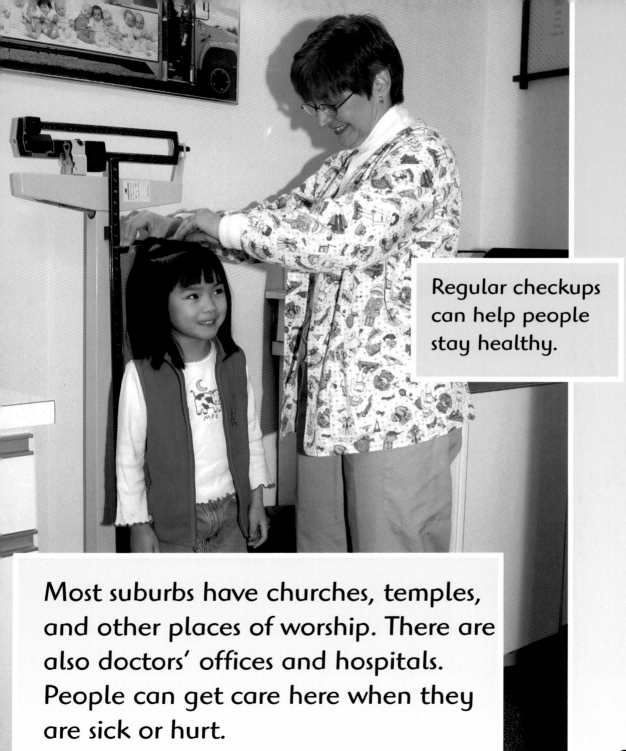

Regular checkups
can help people
stay healthy.

Most suburbs have churches, temples,
and other places of worship. There are
also doctors' offices and hospitals.
People can get care here when they
are sick or hurt.

Having Fun

Many suburbs have parks, ball fields, bike paths, and playgrounds. There may be concert halls where people can hear music. There are usually movie theaters, too.

Many people in suburbs like to play and relax in their own yards.

A suburb's community center may have a pool for people to share.

Suburbs often have **community centers** with gyms, exercise machines, and fun things to do. People also travel to the city for plays, concerts, and sporting events. They may visit **museums** or zoos as well.

The Suburb Comes Together

People may **recycle** or pick up trash to keep their **neighborhoods** clean.

People in suburbs often work together. They collect food, clothing, and other items for those in need. They raise money and run special programs to help others.

People in suburbs also have fun together. They may have parties, parades, and other special events. People share food, music, games, and fun. All these things make suburbs great places to live.

People have fun getting to know each other at neighborhood parties.

Glossary

ATM bank machine that people use to put in and take out money

branch small part of something bigger

carpool ride together in one car

city hall building where a city's leaders meet

community group of people who live in one area, or the area where they live

community center place where people in a community can gather to do activities

court place where people hear and decide matters of law

emergency sudden event that makes you act quickly

farmers' market place where people sell things that were grown or made on farms

government people who make rules for a community, or the rules they make

mall shopping center with many different kinds of stores in one building

metropolitan area area that includes a city and the communities around it

museum place where special or important items are shown

neighborhood small area of a city or town

patrol travel through an area to keep it safe

public transportation ways of travel that are organized and that everyone can use

recycle collect items such as paper, plastic, metal, and glass so that they can be used again

strip mall one long building divided into many different stores

subway train that runs underground

town house house that is joined to the houses next to it, usually in a row

More Books to Read

Caseley, Judith. *On the Town: A Community Adventure.* New York: Greenwillow, 2002.

Kalman, Bobbie. *What Is a Community?: from A to Z.* New York: Crabtree Publishing, 2000.

Turnbauer, Lisa. *Living in a Suburb.* Mankato, Minn.: Capstone Press, 2005.

Index